I'm just a dancer

I'm just a dancer

J. Jansen

Author J. Jansen
Cover design: J. Jansen
ISBN: 9789402102512

Fellow travelers

Why are people afraid
Of showing who they are
What's wrong by showing
Bright colors from within?
It's common for us
To put on a face, a mask to hide
Not seeing is not hurting
Here I dare to show

My deepest thoughts and feelings
Not hidden, or stored
In profound words I write
Showing them to those I respect
Pity those who stay behind
Putting humanity in boxes
Trapped by their own fear
Only able to give calculated responses
To become robotic people

Sometimes I'm ashamed
For crying in public amongst people
With no reason at all, being stared at
But this seems to be my path
It's my weakness and my blessing
This I tell you, this I write for you
Because you're my fellow travelers
Who accompany me on today's journey

Clouds in my head

No more fear of letting go
Gone are the clouds in my head
Somehow it's easier
To live and act in despair
Then sense and praise the good
Make the change you want to see
Life's solutions are yours
You only have to find the key
To answers you already know

The holy man

The holy man spoke
And all men stood still
Only silence remained
Where once was noise

Carried by the wind
His words were spread
While birds were singing
In trees above

After his last word
Nothing....
No whisper, no talking
All remained quiet

Like little seeds
In fertile ground
They embraced the words
Which he planted

Ship of dreams

In my dreams
She takes me
Across the sea
To the promised land

Upon the waves I sail
Carried by the wind
To this ancient land
Where nature calls

Calls my name out loud
Yes, she takes me
And I must go
For my boat awaits

Restless I awake
Impatient and determined
I go across the sea
To find my paradise

A forgotten dream

Hold on is what I say
You're all I'll ever need
I tell you every day
That my heart will bleed
So please stop screaming
We can never part
Not even in my dream
Though you break my heart

Although light turns dark
And birds have lost their song
Can't wash away your mark
Here is where I still belong
So please stop screaming
We will never part
Not even in your dream
Though I break your heart

We were meant to be
All this time we knew
We loved so intensely
As only few people ever do
So please stop screaming
We shouldn't ever part
Not even in our dream
Though we break each other's heart

We are no longer together
Going our own way we do

Always know I went as far
As your love allowed me to
So please stop screaming
We were already apart
Even before we started dreaming
Because we didn't give our whole hearts

Wandering

This day slowly passes by
Hours still dragging on
Where do I go from here
Doesn't anyone hear my song?

As I wander in the forest
Crying all through the night
With silver flowing tears
Where's the one I've left behind?

Suddenly I see a glow
A lighter presence appearing
From a distance, Oh so far
To reach my skin; I do not fear

Now I see beautiful colors
Dark moods just turn into innocence
The sun warms up the earth
As a sign of my bright existence

Our script of life

Our script of life
Doesn't reveal its secrets
We balance on a thin wire
I'm just a dancer like you

Your name

Usually I'm myself
No one tells me if I'm wrong
Now I'm lost in the dark
Can't find where I belong
Have to find the answer
I long for your name

The path which I follow
Seems to me all too clear
Still I can't find you
Everything disappears
Vanishes in a crowd
I long for your name

Why can't I find you
I search everywhere
Just talking to strangers
But they don't care
Desperate as I am
I long for your name

Suddenly you're there
In an unexpected place
Not knowing if it's real
I search for your face
To see eyes full of promise
I long for your name

A brief moment

Nothing more to be said
A whisper in the wind
Which I never will forget
Finally we can be one
I whisper your name

Inspiration

Inspiration is given not only
To the wisest of men
Who discover pi and gravity
Nor is it stored in large buildings
Amongst divine manuscripts
And holy artifacts under glass
It is also found in the minds
Of the blind who can see

Children's dreams

When children stop dreaming
The earth stops breathing
I'm asking on behalf of all mankind
To let them play in peace
So they regain hope
And start to dream again

The stars

Not allowed to wander on my own
Everything is just the same
With every person in a stupid role
I seem to be living in a chess game

Inside my own tiny circle
Grown with the standard way of life
Follow the path which is decided
The stars can tell me why

What lies beneath the horizon?
Perhaps more secrets unsolved
Are there creatures just like us
Pure, beautiful and deeply involved

Our superior behavior is ignorance
A defense weapon of some kind
To protect our way of living
Just like the centuries we left behind

Inside our own tiny little circle
Grown with the standard way of life
Follow the predestined path
The stars can tell us why

Imagine a planet in some other time
With two moons or three if you'd like
Could you believe this only by instinct
Or are you depending on a government lie

Wear ordinary clothes every day
Eat at the same time as all your neighbors do
As if you are a number instead of a person
Obediently laughing when they tell you to

Inside your own tiny little circle
Grown with the standard way of life
Follow the predestined path
The stars can tell you why

Early life wasn't difficult or complex
Look at the stars and remember that day
No pollution or lost species of any kind
Everything you needed was here to stay

All rivers filled with fish and clean water
So tasteful and juicy as the fruits used to be
Rainforest with no threat of decimation
What kind of paradise would this be

What if we break free of our tiny little circles
To create a new standard way of life
A new path for the coming years
With the stars to be our guide.

Yes, the stars should be our guide....

Phoenix

Opening my soul
Some secrets are revealed
They were so well kept
Almost preserved forever
Starting from childhood
Each time a layer of dust
Landed on the one before

They seem to disorder
My safe life which I'm in
Don't know how to let go
Without being a frightened child
The labyrinth is closing in
And I'm standing in doubt
It's time to let the hunger out

Uncertain is the present
For the time is here
To keep my head up
Go forward through the storm
Despite some people
Judgments of everyone
To become my true self

Silence

Silence
Nothing left to say
Nothing to be heard
All has faded away

Away is the laughter
Away is the sound
Away is the love
We all kicked it out

Out of our streets
Out of our hearts
Out of our cities
We stay and watch

Watch the misery
Watch the sorrow
Watch the shame
Still........ in silence

Beautiful day

I close my eyes and know
Everything seems good today
A complete person people say
But nobody notices the truth
About feelings and thoughts
Which are floating

I'm walking in the streets
Searching for nothing at all
Suddenly I feel a shiver
And turn around to see
Nothing is there
But something's surrounding me

I sit down on the ground nearby
Where grass and trees grow
A light stroke of my hand
Makes me realize how fragile things can be
And without them
All seems lost and so cold to me

I can't explain
This moment of wonder
City's sounds all around me
But I feel at ease
Calm and clear in mind
While I lie down and look at the sky

What will happen to my world

And to the people in the streets
With their own story
Can we take control again
To overcome and be happy
Before a new year begins?

The crack of dawn

At the crack of dawn
She wakes me up
Standing beside my bed
Feeling troubled and alone

She can't explain
Doesn't know how to say
There is a yearning
Nothing makes it go away

Memories she doesn't recall
At least of that moment in time
It's more an absent feeling
She senses every now and then

Always searching
Trying to fill up the hole
She doesn't yet understand
But one day she will

One day she must....

An unexpected story

I stood in front of my teacher
Like a servant before her king
We started a conversation
About a little thing

I asked him some questions
And he started to smile
He shook his head and said
Wait just a little while

You're impatient and young
But your heart is already at peace
How did you manage this?
Answer me if you please

I looked up at him
And stared in his twinkling eyes
He really did know me
That was a lovely surprise

I felt moved and inspired
To hear those words from him
From the one who was loved
So I whispered "where do I begin?"

But suddenly a fog appeared
Confused, I started to scream
Then he spoke the magical words:
"I'm just a figure in your dream"

Beautiful you

We took the car
last Saturday morning
It seemed a normal day
For a short visit
Friends and I just went away

We were laughing
Having a wonderful time
Stepped inside a megastore
To listen to music
Nothing else mattered no more

A warm glow came through
And even before I saw
Who was looking at me
I felt my heart
Pounding loud and feeling free

A beautiful face
Full of love and tenderness
Was laughing again, taking
Away pain and misery
My heart opened up its door

It could only be
The dearest friend I had lost
So many lonely years ago
Who belonged to me
Until sadly enough I had to go

I hurried back outside
And just as she started to cry
I embraced her tenderly
Then she said with a glorious smile:
"A new beginning was always meant to be"

Childish eyes

Near the fireplace
She sits in a wooden chair
Holding a puppet in her hand
I see an absence of mind
In her childish eyes

She has left the here and now
To see long lost faces
Now and then her high voice
Calls for her mother
Who went to buy some fresh milk

Living amongst memories
Not hearing other's sounds
Just humming children's songs
How can we break through
If we have any questions

We don't know, or understand
How to live in isolation
Only remembering the past
Some sense of recognition
A strange kind of déjà vu

I'm watching her enjoy
Blowing out invisible candles,
With a beautiful smile
She looks happy and alive
Just celebrating being five

Fortune

Fortune is not only assuming
The expected and respected
But also gathering wisdom
By seeing and exploring the invisible

Anger

Feeling frustrated
So all alone
Friends keep saying
Let us take you home

Nothing they say
Can stop this pain
I can't stay
I'm going away

My baby's lost
I'm incomplete
No matter what
I suffer defeat

Telling myself
A record in my mind
Unleash the anger
You left behind

How can it be
Why didn't you stay
Our moment of love
Just went away

Put on my coat
I start to walk
Without a light
I follow the dark

Cups of joy

Let the cups of joy
Be emptied in the sea
Where it's taken by the waves
Upon the hour will come
A time when it shall reach
All desperate shores
So there will be
Hope and faith again
Among those who are lost
To water their plants
With a cup of wisdom

Never ending story

Using my eyes
I still don't see
Guess that's the story
Of the never-ending one
There's no beginning
For there's no end
The circle of life
Never stops

My lovely stranger

All those painful tears
Rolling down my cheek
Are a sign of love
They don't make me weak
Everything is different
But still the same
No one can tell
Only I know your name

Dreams of a child

A nightmare becomes real
When children have no future
Without future no life
Without life only death
Return to life is
Return to the future
Returning to the future is
Return to the child
A child without borders
Creates wonderful dreams

Rat race

There's nothing left to say
No more rat race to play
The lights are going out
For the first time there's no doubt
Putting away all I've collected
Reaching for those whom I've neglected
A blooming heart overrules my mind
My darkest thoughts I leave behind
Away is my sorrow and endless misery
Life has become my true destiny

Friend

Hey friend
What's happening to you
You've changed in many ways
I don't know
Who you are anymore
A stranger with a familiar face
That's what it seems

We stood together
Through sorrow and pain
The wrong people
The wrong places
Still we were the same

I wish I'd known
How to make you come back
To become the one
You were before
But I don't know how to reach
Or make you understand
That I miss you

My life makes a turn
Away from you it seems
Don't want to leave
But I have to move on
Wish you were by my side
To see the things
We haven't seen before

But I don't know how to reach
Or make you understand
That I miss you

Mourning

So much to mourn
This enormous pain hurts
What has become
Of this world
If we can't trust our father
The one who should
Protect and love us
But instead makes us cry
Gives us pain and death
Why can't this be stopped
Before it's too late
And now two lovely children
Have gone away
Leaving their mother
With nothing to live for....

Music in my mind

Music in my mind
Makes me forget the past
While floating in the sky
Don't care about the rest
All troubles long gone
No more words today
This moment's mine
Nothing else to say
I see the little people
staring up at the sky
They look so funny to me
I am the last to deny
I'm starting this last journey
The world lies at my feet
My makers' endless love
Makes me feel complete

Lessons of life

A tear on my cheek
Some regrets still hurt
What can I do
To stop this negative turn

When do these tears stop falling
What will the future bring
Perhaps a hunger for knowledge
Or simply the need to believe

Where did it all go wrong
When did I lose faith
What were my intentions
Am I the one to blame

The shame that I'm feeling
Memories of so long ago
Stupid decisions which I've made
The lies that I have lived on

What if people told me
To leave and never look back
Would I find myself in the dark
With no lights to guide me back

Where do I find new hope
When will it all go right
Whatever the future will bring
I am the one who must fight

The lessons I've learned
Are very special to me
The difference between right and wrong
Lessons for the one I'd like to be

A new beginning

So many colors
So many faces
So many sounds
So many expectations
It's all happening
The time is now
I have to start
Today somehow
Welcome beautiful life!!

Modern days

The modern days we are living in
Have so much to give
Unlimited adventures
All around the globe
Distance doesn't exist anymore
Modern technology is here
To help us take steps
So we can interact every day
With those from afar
Who have a similar heart

Hope

Going away is everything
That I want right now
To put my diary in my bag
My phone in my pocket
To throw the keys away
And close the door behind me

These battles of words
Are turning laughter into tears
All we do is hurt
So much heartache
I have to go away
To save what's between us

But your love haunts me
It never leaves me alone
You appear in tiny things
Unexpected every time
The longing drives me crazy
And I almost start to cry

But if I do I'd be lost
And nothing will be changed
Overwhelmed by near madness
I close my eyes and feel
Your love embrace me
It's impossible to let go

I know this last goodbye

Is the hardest of all
Why surrender
If it leaves me alone?
My soul will lose its twin
And darkness fill my heart

That's why I hope
Hope and pray that you
Will reach out to me
So we can turn around
Turn the earth around
And try again, again....

When my heart speaks...

It's because
Various thoughts
Are filled with emotion
Like the waves
They come and go
Facts and feelings
Battle with each other
To create order
In a chaotic mind

Venice

Gondolas in the water
Create a peaceful sight
People around me
Walk through time every day
A Venetian
Is a tourist in his hometown
Amongst the people
He feels he is abroad
Is there anything left
Of their glorious history
Some small part
Which no one knows
Or is that the price for civilization

The pulse of love

I still love you
I still need you
I feel no regret not even for a day
Your love scares my dark moments away

Just now I'm barely awake
As I'm starting to think
My head is still not to clear
But you're beside me, you're still near

Between little kisses
Your voice whispers to me
Every touch of your hand
Make me simply understand

You still love me
You still need me
You feel no regret not even for a day
My love scares your dark moments away

So don't leave me or say goodbye
I'd turn cold and into stone if you did
Stay with me, that's what I ask of you
We belong together and you know it's true

To love in good times and in bad
That's what we're planning to do
I believe our love rises above
Because when I look into your eyes I see love

We still love each other
We still need each other
We feel no regrets not even for a day
Our love scares the dark moments away

A mother's song

I want to write a song of love
Simply just for you
To share my deepest feelings
As I've planned for so long to do

While I sit here doing this
The words don't seem right
Because all I talk about is me
I don't even ask if you're alright

So tell me how you feel inside
Straight from me to you
As mother and daughter
Sharing hearts as we used to do

For the day will come without warning
Too fast to even say goodbye
So let us make a promise today
When it does to take a look at the sky

To remember the one who leaves
Not only in devastation and fear
But also celebrating a loving life
With memories of laughing and a tear

Because we give each other love
From my birth until that day
We know it won't last forever
But we love each other in a beautiful way

www.ingramcontent.com/pod-product-compliance
Lightning Source LLC
Chambersburg PA
CBHW060628030426
42337CB00018B/3248